60

FARRAR
STRAUS
GIROUX

HORSE LATITUDES

HORSE LATITUDES

PAUL MULDOON

FARRAR, STRAUS AND GIROUX

NEW YORK

FARRAR, STRAUS AND GIROUX
18 West 18th Street, New York 10011

Copyright © 2006 by Paul Muldoon
All rights reserved
Distributed in Canada by Douglas & McIntyre Ltd.
Printed in the United States of America
Published in 2006 by Farrar, Straus and Giroux
First paperback edition, 2007

The Library of Congress has cataloged the hardcover edition as follows:
Muldoon, Paul.
    Horse latitudes / Paul Muldoon.— 1st ed.
        p.   cm.
    Poems.

    I. Title.

PR6063.U367H67 2006
821'.914—dc22

                                        2006000306

Paperback ISBN-13: 978-0-374-53101-0
Paperback ISBN-10: 0-374-53101-3

Designed by Gretchen Achilles

www.fsgbooks.com

IN MEMORY OF

MAUREEN MULDOON

1953–2005

CONTENTS

Horse Latitudes	3
Tithonus	22
Bob Dylan at Princeton, November 2000	24
The Biddy Boys	25
Alba	26
Soccer Moms	28
As Your Husband Looks Up to Our Window	.30
The Procedure	31
The Treaty	32
Eggs	33
At Least They Weren't Speaking French	35
The Old Country	38
The Outlier	47
It Is What It Is	49
Turtles	50
Flags and Emblems	51
90 Instant Messages to Tom Moore	53
Riddle	76
Turkey Buzzards	78
Starlings, Broad Street, Trenton, 2003	82
The Coyote	83
Now Pitching Himself Like a Forlorn Hope	84
Perdu	85
The Landing	86
The Mountain Is Holding Out	87

Medley for Morin Khur   89

Glaucus   91

The Last Time I Saw Chris   92

Hedge School   94

Sillyhow Stride: *In Memory of Warren Zevon*   95

Acknowledgments   107

HORSE LATITUDES

HORSE LATITUDES

BEIJING

I could still hear the musicians
cajoling those thousands of clay
horses and horsemen through the squeeze
when I woke beside Carlotta.
Life-size, also. Also terra-cotta.
The sky was still a terra-cotta frieze
over which her grandfather still held sway
with the set square, fretsaw, stencil,
plumb line, and carpenter's pencil
his grandfather brought from Roma.
Proud-fleshed Carlotta. Hypersarcoma.
For now our highest ambition
was simply to bear the light of the day
we had once been planning to seize.

BAGINBUN

The Nashville skyline's hem and haw
as the freebooters who freeboot
through their contractual mire and murk,
like Normans stampeding dozens
of cows into their Norse-Irish cousins,
were balking now at this massive breastwork
they themselves had thrown up. The pile of toot
on a mirror. The hip-hirple
of a white horse against purple.
Age-old traductions I could trace
from freebasers pretending they freebase
to this inescapable flaw
hidden by Carlotta's close-knit wet suit
like a heart-wound by a hauberk.

BANNOCKBURN

Though he was mounted on a cob
rather than a warhorse, the Bruce
still managed to sidestep a spear
from Henry de Bohun and tax
de Bohun's poll with his broad-based poleax
and leave de Bohun's charger somewhat leer.
Her grandfather had yet to find a use
for the two-timing partisan
his grandfather brought man-to-man
against all those Ferdinandies
until he saw it might come in handy
for whacking the thingammybobs
off pine and fir, off pine and fir and spruce
and all such trees as volunteer.

BERWICK-UPON-TWEED

Off the elm, the ancient pollard
that a Flemish painter might love,
that comes to shun the attention
of its headstrong days, so is proof
against the storm that takes its neighbor's roof.
Her *nonno* collects his pension
knowing that when push really came to shove
he had it within him to wrap
his legs in puttees and backslap
those pack mules down that moonlit deck,
Carlotta now wearing a halter-neck
under the long-sleeved, high-collared
wet suit whereof . . . whereof . . . whereof . . . whereof
I needs must again make mention.

BLAYE

Her wet suit like a coat of mail
worn by a French knight from the time
a knight could still cause a ruction
by direct-charging his rouncy,
when an Englishman's home was his bouncy
castle, when abduction and *seduction*
went hand in glove. Now Carlotta would climb
from the hotel pool in Nashville,
take off her mask, and set a spill
to a Gauloise as one might set
a spill to the fuse of a falconet
and the walls of her chest assail.
The French, meanwhile, were still struggling to prime
their weapons of mass destruction.

BOSWORTH FIELD

It was clear now, through the pell-mell
of bombard- and basilisk-mist,
that the Stanleys had done the dirt
on him and taken Henry's side.
Now Richard's very blood seemed to have shied
away from him, seemed to sputter and spurt
like a falcon sheering off from his wrist
as he tried to distance himself
from the same falchioneer who'd pelf
the crown from his blood-matted brow
and hang it in a tree. Less clear was how
he'd managed not to crack the shell
of the pigeon egg the size of a cyst
he'd held so close inside his shirt.

BLACKWATER FORT

As I had held Carlotta close
that night we watched some Xenophon
embedded with the 5th Marines
in the old Sunni Triangle
make a half-assed attempt to untangle
the ghastly from the price of gasoline.
There was a distant fanfaron
in the Nashville sky, where the wind
had now drawn itself up and pinned
on her breast a Texaco star.
"Why," Carlotta wondered, "the House of *Tar*?
Might it have to do with the gross
imports of crude oil Bush will come clean on
only when the Tigris comes clean?"

BENBURB

Those impromptu chevaux-de-frise
into which they galloped full tilt
and impaled themselves have all but
thrown off their balance the banner-
bearing Scots determined to put manners
on the beech mast– and cress- and hazelnut-
eating Irish. However jerry-built,
those chevaux-de-frise have embogged
the horses whose manes they had hogged
so lovingly and decked with knots
of heather, horses rooted to the spots
on which they go down on their knees
as they unwind their shoulder plaids and kilts,
the checkered careers of their guts.

BOYNE

The blood slick from the horse slaughter
I could no longer disregard
as Carlotta surfaced like barm.
My putting her through her paces
as she kicked and kicked against the traces
like a pack mule kicking from a yardarm
before it fell, heehaw, in the dockyard.
A banner's frittering tassel
or deflating bouncy castle
was something to which she paid heed
whereas that vision of a milk-white steed
drinking from a tub of water
and breathing hard, breathing a little hard,
had barely set off an alarm.

BLENHEIM

Small birds were sounding the alert
as I followed her unladen
steed through a dell so dark and dank
she might have sported the waders
her grandfather had worn at the nadir
of his career, scouring the Outer Banks
for mummichog and menhaden.
Those weeks and months in the doldrums
coming back as he ran his thumb
along an old venetian blind
in the hope that something might come to mind,
that he might yet animadvert
the maiden name of that Iron Maiden
on which he was drawing a blank.

BUNKER HILL

Carlotta took me in her arms
as a campfire gathers a branch
to itself, her mouth a cauter
set to my bleeding bough, heehaw.
Her grandfather sterilizing his saw
in a tub of 100-proof firewater,
a helper standing by to stanch
the bleeding in some afterlife.
No looking daggers at the knife.
She'd meet the breast-high parapet
with the nonchalance, the no fucking sweat
of a slightly skanky schoolmarm
though the surgeon was preparing to ganch
her like What's-his-face's Daughter.

BRANDYWINE

I crouched in my own Little Ease
by the pool at the Vanderbilt
where Carlotta crouched, sputter-sput,
just as she had in the scanner
when the nurse, keen-sighted as a lanner,
picked out a tumor like a rabbit scut
on dark ground. It was as if a fine silt,
white sand or silicate, had clogged
her snorkel, her goggles had fogged,
and Carlotta surfaced like flot
to be skimmed off some great cast-iron pot
as garble is skimmed off, or lees
painstakingly drained by turnings and tilts
from a man-size barrel or butt.

BADLI-KE-SERAI

Pork barrels. *Pork* butts. The wide-screen
surround sound of a massed attack
upon the thin red cellulose
by those dust- or fust- or must-cells
that cause the tears to well and well and well.
At which I see him turning up his nose
as if he'd bitten on a powder-pack
like yet another sad Sepoy
who won't fall for the British ploy
of greasing with ham the hammer
or smoothing over Carlotta's grammar:
"*On which* . . . *On which* Bush will come clean."
Her grandfather a man who sees no lack
of manhood in the lachrymose.

BULL RUN

While some think there's nothing more rank
than the pool that's long stood aloof
from the freshet, I loved the smell
of sweat and blood and, *sí*, horse dung
Carlotta shouldered like an Aqua-Lung
as she led me now through that dewy dell
and spread her House of Tartan waterproof.
As we lay there I could have sworn,
as I stared through unruffled thorns
that were an almost perfect fit
to each side of the gravel pit
where she and I'd tried to outflank
each other, I traced the mark of a hoof
(or horseshoe) in her fontanelle.

BRONKHORSTSPRUIT

I traced the age-old traduction
of a stream through a thorn thicket
as a gush from a farthingale.
Skeffington's Daughter. *Skeffington.*
Attention. Shun. Attention. Shun. Shun. Shun.
We lay in a siding between two rails
and watched an old white horse cross the picket
of himself and trek through the scrub
to drink from an iron-hooped tub
with the snore-snort of a tuba.
His winkers and bellyband said scuba,
while his sudden loss of suction
Carlotta knew meant a pump whose clicket's
failed in the way a clicket fails.

BASRA

"The way to relieve the tension
on the line to a windjammer
is to lubricate the bollard
so it's always a little slack . . ."
Her *nonno* giving us the inside track
on how the mule drivers whooped and hollered
on the dock. No respite from his yammer
on boundlessness being a bind
and the most insidious kind
of censorship self-censorship
while he took Carlotta for a quick whip
through conjugation, declension,
and those other "crannies of the crammer"
in which she'd been "quite unscholared."

BAZENTIN

As I was bringing up her rear
a young dragoon would cock a snook
at the gunners raking the knob
of High Wood. Tongue like a scaldy
in a nest. Hadn't a Garibaldi
what might lie behind that low-level throb
like a niggle in her appointment book.
Dust? Fust? Must? The dragoon nonplussed
by his charger taking the rust
and, despite her recalcitrance,
Carlotta making a modest advance
when the thought of a falchioneer
falling to with his two-faced reaping hook
now brought back her grandfather's job.

BEERSHEBA

Now summoned also the young Turk
who had suddenly arisen
from that great pile of toot, heehaw,
as from one of Beersheba's wells.
Like the sail that all of a sudden swells
on the yawl that all of a sudden yaws,
a wind finding meaning in a mizzen
and toppling a bouncy castle.
Her grandfather fain to wrastle
each pack mule to a rubber mat
whereat . . . whereat . . . whereat . . . whereat . . . whereat . . .
he would eftsoons get down to work,
reaching into its wide-open wizen
while a helper clamped back its jaws.

BURMA

Her grandfather's job was to cut
the vocal cords of each pack mule
with a single, swift excision,
a helper standing by to wrench
the mule's head fiercely to one side and drench
it with hooch he'd kept since Prohibition.
"Why," Carlotta wondered, "that fearsome tool?
Was it for fear the mules might bray
and give their position away?"
At which I see him thumb the shade
as if he were once more testing a blade
and hear the two-fold snapping shut
of his four-fold, brass-edged carpenter's rule:
"And give *away* their *position*."

TITHONUS

Not the day-old cheep of a smoke detector on the blink
in what used to be the root cellar,
or the hush-hush of all those drowsy syrups
against their stoppers

in the apothecary chest
at the far end of your grandmother's attic,
nor the "my sweet, my sweet"
of ice branch frigging ice branch,

nor the jinkle-jink
of your great-grandfather, the bank teller
who kept six shots of medicinal (he called it "therap-
utraquist") whiskey like six stacks of coppers

stacked against him by the best
and brightest of the American Numismatic
Society from the other side of 155th Street,
nor the in-the-silence-after-the-horse-avalanche

spur-spink
heard by your great-great-grandfather, the Rebel yeller
who happened to lose a stirrup
and come a cropper

at the very start of the Confederate offensive in the west,
nor even the phatic
whittering of your great-great-grandmother ("such a good *seat*")
whose name was, of all things, Blanche,

nor again the day-old cheep of a smoke detector on the blink
in what used to be the root cellar
but what turns out to be the two-thousand-year-old chirrup
of a grasshopper.

BOB DYLAN AT PRINCETON, NOVEMBER 2000

We cluster at one end, one end of Dillon Gym.
"You know what, honey? We call that a homonym."

We cluster at one end, one end of Dillon Gym.
"If it's fruit you're after, you go out on a limb."

That last time in Princeton, that ornery degree,
those seventeen-year locusts hanging off the trees.

That last time in Princeton, that ornery degree,
his absolute refusal to bend the knee.

His last time in Princeton, he wouldn't wear a hood.
Now he's dressed up as some sort of cowboy dude.

That last time in Princeton, he wouldn't wear a hood.
"You know what, honey? We call that disquietude.

It's that self-same impulse that has him rearrange
both 'The Times They Are A-Changin' ' and 'Things Have Changed'

so that everything seems to fall within his range
as the locusts lock in on grain silo and grange."

THE BIDDY BOYS

We've turned a corner in the ancient Barony of Lurg
when we come on six or seven worthies in straw capes and hats.
Their roundy heads are wrapped in muslin.
A geranium, that must be, through the curtained window.

The curtained window of the wake house their Captain now enters.
A white horse bustling under his bustling sheet.
His wooden horse head fitted with some kind of spike.
He pricks a mourner here and a mourner there.

A mourner here and there cries out.
"The Humours of Kesh" played on two fiddles.
A pair of rain-bleached horses standing head to tail.

Standing head to tail like some old married couple.
The geranium of your mouth through that curtained window:
"Things were bad for a long while but now we've turned a corner."

ALBA

I was baffled, baffled as one who wakes
in an open field to find the circus
has pulled up its stakes
and uncovered the Sargasso

of the So-and-Sos' pool,
the pool from which some kid had filled the radiator
of their, drool,
Mercedes-Benz "off-roader,"

the Sargasso where the Big Top
must have stood. Last night the rigging growled
and grunted, clippety-clop,
just as Carlotta

emerged from the duckweed
to announce her name was an anagram
of "oral fucking tact."
I heard that. While the others swam

we lay alongside each other
to gam as whalers gam.
Where we once had made good weather
was now a region of calms

in which the no-can-doers at last did medallions
of veal with hearts of palm,
in which the Arabian stallion
still managed a salaam

despite Carlotta's jettisoning his six mares
in an effort to break the deadlock.
This was the field where our sons and heirs
had been playing Little League

when we met, where she asked me to imagine
a sky grown pale
from *too much* sun.
I imagined it. I imagined, too, the bleached snatch of sail

with a list of putative damages to the So-and-Sos'
Geländewagen, the receipt from Jiffy Lube
for a new radiator hose,
and—a bit like an eel—this equestrienne's whip.

SOCCER MOMS

They remember Gene Chandler topping the charts with "Duke of Earl"
when the boys were set on taking the milk bar's one banquette
and winning their hearts, Mavis and Merle,

as it seemed their hearts might be first to yield,
hearts before minds. Time for stilettos. Time for spivs with shivs.
The time of day when light fails on the field

while their daughters, themselves now tweenie girls,
crowd round a coach for one last tête-à-tête.
They remember Gene Chandler topping the charts with "Duke of Earl"

while the world still reeled
from the anti-Castro Cubans going to sea in a sieve,
as it seemed. Their hearts might be first to yield

if only after forty years of one plain, one purl,
on the sweater they've sweated over for a Bay of Pigs vet,
and winning their hearts, Mavis and Merle,

may now be faintly likelier for a well-heeled
schlub to whom they once wouldn't so much as give
the time of day. When light fails on the field

a schlubster linesman will unfurl
an offside flag that signals some vague threat,
they remember. Gene Chandler topping the charts with "Duke of Earl"

for three weeks only in 1962 might have taught them to shield
themselves against the lives their daughters briefly relive,
as it seemed *their* hearts might be first to yield

to this free kick that forever curls
past the goal-mouth, a ball at once winging into the back of the net
and winning. Their hearts, Mavis and Merle,

hanker for the time when it was not yet revealed
failure's no less literal than figurative,
the time of day when light fails on the field

and gives back a sky more muddy than mother-of-pearl,
so it's with a deepening sense of regret
they remember Gene Chandler topping the charts with "Duke of Earl"
and winning their hearts, Mavis and Merle.

AS YOUR HUSBAND LOOKS UP TO OUR WINDOW

The man who's unwinding the red-and-white-striped awning
of the *boucherie* across the street takes in not the wide-screen Sensurround
on which it might be just now dawning

but the letter box between ham and hock. A reputation for
    simultaneously fawning
upon and fanging the clientele is one of many that hound
the man who's unwinding the red-and-white-striped awning,

his great-grandfather having opened this very store only a year after
    impawning
was banned by the Commune on the grounds there are no grounds
on which it's just. Now dawning

in a home theater near you is the sequel-spawning
realization that mont-de-piété signifies not "piety-mound"
to the man who's unwinding the red-and-white-striped awning

but the methodical deboning and debrowning
of a pig in a poke that's been crowned not once but triple-crowned.
It's just now dawning

on you, as your husband looks up to our window, half-yearning, half-
    yawning,
having at long, long last unwound
the red-and-white-striped awning,
that on him, too, it's just now dawning.

THE PROCEDURE

I

One still wore a wristband from the disco
where we'd flattered each other through the strobe
long before she was of an age to boast
as many tongues as many-tongued Rumor.

II

It dawned as it dawns on San Francisco
on another who rummaged in her robe
and varied the standard-issue tea and toast
with a grapefruit the size of a tumor.

III

Both came to mind last evening when I set
my wedding ring on top of the nightstand
as if I might once again be making

it clear to the pale beauty I was yet
to meet in Madigan's or the Four in Hand
that I was free and ready for taking.

THE TREATY

My grandfather Frank Regan, cross-shanked, his shoulders in a moult,
steadies the buff
of his underparts against the ledge of the chimney bluff
of the mud-walled house in Cullenramer

in which, earlier, he had broken open a bolt
of the sky-stuff
and held it to the failing light, having himself failed to balance Gormley's
    cuffs.
"This Collins," Gormley had wagged, "is a right flimflammer."

Cross-shanked against the chimney bluff, he's sizing up what follows
from our being on the verge
of nation-

hood when another broad-lapelled, swallow-tailed swallow
comes at a clip through the dusk-blue serge
to make some last-minute alterations.

EGGS

I was unpacking a dozen eggs
into the fridge when I noticed a hairline crack
at which I pecked

till at long last I squeezed
into a freshly whitewashed
scullery in Cullenramer. It was all hush-hush

where my mother's mother took a potash rag
to a dozen new-laid eggs
and, balancing a basket on her bike,

pushed off for Dungannon. This was much
before the time a priest would touch
down from the Philippines with a clutch

of game bird eggs
and introduce a whole new strain of fighting cocks.
It would be midnight when my mother's mother got back

from Dungannon, now completely smashed
on hard liquor bought with hard cash,
fuck you, cash on the barrel. It was all hush-hush

as she was taken from a truck
painted matter-of-factly MILK & EGGS
into which they'd bundled her, along with her bike,

for delivery to Cullenramer. It would be all hush-hush
next morning in the whitewashed
scullery where she wrung out the potash

rag and took it to another dozen or so new-laid eggs,
from any one of which I might yet poke
my little beak.

AT LEAST THEY WEREN'T SPEAKING FRENCH

I

At least they weren't speaking French
when my father sat with his brothers and sisters, two of each, on a
    ramshackle bench
at the end of a lane marked by two white stones
and made mouth music as they waited, chilled to the bone

fol-de-rol fol-de-rol fol-de-rol-di-do

for the bus meant to bring their parents back from town.
It came and went. Nothing. One sister was weighed down
by the youngest child. A grocery bag from a town more distant still, in
    troth.
What started as a cough

fol-de-rol fol-de-rol fol-de-rol-di-do

would briefly push him forward to some minor renown,
then shove him back, oddly summery, down
along the trench
to that far-flung realm where, at least, they weren't speaking French.

At least they weren't speaking French
when another brother, twenty-something, stepped on a nail no one had
    bothered to clench
in a plank thrown
halfheartedly from the known to the unknown

fol-de-rol fol-de-rol fol-de-rol-di-do

across a drainage ditch on a building site. His nut-brown arm. His leg nut-
    brown.
That nail sheathed in a fine down
would take no more than a week or ten days to burgeon from the froth
of that piddling little runoff

fol-de-rol fol-de-rol fol-de-rol-di-do

and make of him a green and burning tree. His septicaemia-crown.
Sowans as much as he could manage. Trying to keep that flummery down
as much as any of them could manage. However they might describe the
    stench,
as exhalation, as odor, at least they weren't speaking French.

At least they weren't speaking French
when those twenty-something council workers, one with a winch, the
    other a wrench,
would point my son and me to a long overgrown
lane marked by two faded stones

fol-de-rol fol-de-rol fol-de-rol-di-do

like two white-faced clowns
gaping at the generations who passed between them and set down
bag after grocery bag. Setting them on the table. The newspaper
    tablecloth.
1976. Not the East Tyrone Brigade, not Baader-Meinhof

fol-de-rol fol-de-rol fol-de-rol-di-do

bringing the suggestion of a frown
to those two mummer stones still trying to lie low, trying to keep their
    mummery down
to a bare minimum, two stones that, were they to speak, might blench
as much at their own giving out as our taking in that at least they weren't
    speaking French.

THE OLD COUNTRY

I

Where every town was a tidy town
and every garden a hanging garden.
A half could be had for half a crown.
Every major artery would harden

since every meal was a square meal.
Every clothesline showed a line of undies
yet no house was in dishabille.
Every Sunday took a month of Sundays

till everyone got it off by heart
every start was a bad start
since all conclusions were foregone.

Every wood had its twist of woodbine.
Every cliff its herd of fatalistic swine.
Every runnel was a Rubicon.

II

Every runnel was a Rubicon
and every annual a hardy annual
applying itself like linen to a lawn.
Every glove compartment held a manual

and a map of the roads, major and minor.
Every major road had major roadworks.
Every wishy-washy water diviner
had stood like a bulwark

against something worth standing against.
The smell of incense left us incensed
at the firing of the fort.

Every heron was a presager
of some disaster after which, we'd wager,
every resort was a last resort.

III

Every resort was a last resort
with a harbor that harbored an old grudge.
Every sale was a selling short.
There were those who simply wouldn't budge

from the *Dandy* to the *Rover*.
That shouting was the shouting
but for which it was all over—
the weekend, I mean, we set off on an outing

with the weekday train timetable.
Every tower was a tower of Babel
that graced each corner of a bawn

where every lookout was a poor lookout.
Every rill had its unflashy trout.
Every runnel was a Rubicon.

IV

Every runnel was a Rubicon
where every ditch was a last ditch.
Every man was "a grand wee mon"
whose every pitch was another sales pitch

now every boat was a burned boat.
Every cap was a cap in hand.
Every coat a trailed coat.
Every band was a gallant band

across the broken bridge
and broken ridge after broken ridge
where you couldn't beat a stick with a big stick.

Every straight road was a straight up speed trap.
Every decision was a snap.
Every cut was a cut to the quick.

V

Every cut was a cut to the quick
when the weasel's twist met the weasel's tooth
and Christ was somewhat impolitic
in branding as "weasels fighting in a hole," forsooth,

the petrol smugglers back on the old sod
when a vendor of red diesel
for whom every rod was a green rod
reminded one and all that the weasel

was nowhere to be found in that same quarter.
No mere mortar could withstand a ten-inch mortar.
Every hope was a forlorn hope.

So it was that the defenders
were taken in by their own blood splendour.
Every slope was a slippery slope.

VI

Every slope was a slippery slope
where every shave was a very close shave
and money was money for old rope
where every grave was a watery grave

now every boat was, again, a burned boat.
Every dime-a-dozen rat a dime-a-dozen drowned rat
except for the whitrack, or stoat,
which the very Norsemen had down pat

as a weasel-word
though we know their speech was rather slurred.
Every time was time in the nick

just as every nick was a nick in time.
Every unsheathed sword was somehow sheathed in rime.
Every cut was a cut to the quick.

VII

Every cut was a cut to the quick
what with every feather a feather to ruffle.
Every whitrack was a whitterick.
Everyone was in a right kerfuffle

when from his hob some hobbledehoy
would venture the whitterick was a curlew.
Every wall was a wall of Troy
and every hunt a hunt in the purlieu

of a demesne so out of bounds
every hound might have been a hellhound.
At every lane end stood a milk churn

whose every dent was a sign of indenture
to some pig wormer or cattle drencher.
Every point was a point of no return.

VIII

Every point was a point of no return
for those who had signed the Covenant in blood.
Every fern was a maidenhair fern
that gave every eye an eyeful of mud

ere it was plucked out and cast into the flame.
Every rowan was a mountain ash.
Every swath-swathed mower made of his graft a game
and the hay sash

went to the kemper best fit to kemp.
Every secretary was a temp
who could shift shape

like the river goddesses Banna and Boann.
Every two-a-penny maze was, at its heart, Minoan.
Every escape was a narrow escape.

IX

Every escape was a narrow escape
where every stroke was a broad stroke
of an ax on a pig nape.
Every pig was a pig in a poke

though it scooted once through the Diamond
so unfalt—so unfalteringly.
The threshold of pain was outlimened
by the bar raised at high tea

now every scone was a drop scone.
Every ass had an ass's jawbone
that might itself drop from grin to girn.

Every malt was a single malt.
Every pillar was a pillar of salt.
Every point was a point of no return.

X

Every point was a point of no return
where to make a mark was to overstep the mark.
Every brae had its own braw burn.
Every meadow had its meadowlark

that stood in for the laverock.
Those Norse had tried fjord after fjord
to find a tight wee place to dock.
When he made a scourge of small whin cords,

Christ drove out the moneylenders
and all the other bitter-enders
when the thing to have done was take up the slack.

Whin was to furze as furze was to gorse.
Every hobbledehoy had his hobbledyhobbyhorse.
Every track was an inside track.

XI

Every track was an inside track
where every horse had the horse sense
to know it was only a glorified hack.
Every graineen of gratitude was immense

and every platitude a familiar platitude.
Every kemple of hay was a kemple tossed in the air
by a haymaker in a hay feud.
Every chair at the barn dance a musical chair

given how every paltry poltroon
and his paltry dog could carry a tune
yet no one would carry the can

any more than Samson would carry the temple.
Every spinal column was a collapsing stemple.
Every flash was a flash in the pan.

XII

Every flash was a flash in the pan
and every border a herbaceous border
unless it happened to be *an*
herbaceous border as observed by the *Recorder*

or recorded by the *Observer*.
Every widdie stemmed from a willow bole.
Every fervor was a religious fervor
by which we'd fly the godforsaken hole

into which we'd been flung by it.
Every pit was a bottomless pit
out of which every pig needed a piggyback.

Every cow had subsided in its subsidy.
Biddy winked at Paddy and Paddy winked at Biddy.
Every track was an inside track.

XIII

Every track was an inside track
and every job an inside job.
Every whitterick had been a whitrack
until, from his hobbledehob,

that hobbledehobbledehoy
had insisted the whitterick was a curlew.
But every boy was still "one of the boys"
and every girl "ye girl ye"

for whom every dance was a last dance
and every chance a last chance
and every letdown a terrible letdown

from the days when every list was a laundry list
in that old country where, we reminisced,
every town was a tidy town.

THE OUTLIER

I

In Armagh or Tyrone
I fell between two stones.

In Armagh or Tyrone
on a morning in June
I fell between two stones.

In Armagh or Tyrone
on a morning in June
in 1951
I fell between two stones.

In Armagh or Tyrone
on a morning in June
in 1951
I fell between two stones
that raised me as their own.

II

I had one eye, just one,
they prised and propped open.

I had one eye, just one,
they prised and propped open
like a Fomorian's.

I had one eye, just one,
they prised and propped open
like a Fomorian's
with a fire-toughened pine.

I had one eye, just one,
they prised and propped open
like a Fomorian's
so all I looked upon
would itself turn to stone.

IT IS WHAT IT IS

It is what it is, the popping underfoot of the Bubble Wrap
in which Asher's new toy came,
popping like bladder wrack on the foreshore
of a country toward which I've been rowing
for fifty years, my peeping from behind a tamarind
at the peeping ox and ass, the flyer for a pantomime,
the inlaid cigarette box, the shamrock-painted jug,
the New Testament bound in red leather
lying open, Lordie, on her lap
while I mull over the rules of this imperspicuous game
that seems to be missing one piece, if not more.
Her voice at the gridiron coming and going
as if snatched by a sea wind.
My mother. Shipping out for good. For good this time.
The game. The plaything spread on the rug.
The fifty years I've spent trying to put it together.

TURTLES

A cubit-wide turtle acting the bin lid
by the side of the canal
conjures those Belfast nights I lay awake, putting in a bid
for the police channel
as lid bangers gave the whereabouts
of armored cars and petrol bombers lit one flare
after another. So many of those former sentries and scouts
have now taken up the lyre
I can't be sure of what is and what is not.
The water, for example, has the look of tin.
Nor am I certain, given their ability to smell the rot
once the rot sets in,
that turtles have not been enlisted by some police forces
to help them recover corpses.

FLAGS AND EMBLEMS

What to make of your quickie
with some moonlighting Provo or Stickie
who did you over, whoah, did you over,
till your blue-black hickey

Riddle-me-O
Riddle-me-O

ran like mascara?
Or the former members of Tara
who lured you into their new Land Rover
with a couple of ex-Paras

Riddle-me-O
Riddle-me-O

turned paper hangers
and dumped you in a cornfield sangar
(that little hip trench lined with stover
to soften the blow to gangbangers)

Riddle-me-O
Riddle-me-O

like a deer dumped in her own numbles?
Not even the fee-fie-fo-fumble
of a giant cattle drover
with whom you had a little rough and tumble

Riddle-me-O
Riddle-me-O

amid a roundabout's right-as-rain azaleas
can account for the regalia
with its leitmotif of a four-leaf clover
you've worn each year at the great Terminalia

O-riddle-me-O
Riddle-me-riddle-me-O.

90 INSTANT MESSAGES TO TOM MOORE

I

Jim-jams and whim-whams
where the whalers still heave to
for a gammy-gam.

II

Yet another isle
full of noises. Feral hogs.
The turn of turnstiles.

III

Hamilton. Tweeds? Tux?
Baloney? Abalone?
Flux, Tom. Constant flux.

IV

Cough? What's with the cough?
The balls with which a papaw
tries to palm us off.

V

The Big House, you see,
still stands, though now the *tenants*
are the absentees.

VI

Good Friday. We fly
a kite over Bermuda.
Our cross in the sky.

VII

The last of the pod
of sperm whales beached on Nonsuch
turns to the auld sod.

VIII

The black *W*
on the cicada's wings? War.
Hence the ballyhoo.

IX

Hence the strange rapport
between the purple tube sponge
and all it abhors.

X

Here you'd catalogue
each undersea smash-and-grab.
Fog. Grog. Waterlog.

XI

I soar with Sony
and Fleetwood Mac's "Albatross,"
a wide-winged goney.

XII

On a page of straw
torn from the Book of Durrow
a hog snores. Pshaw, pshaw.

XIII

Longtail lieutenants
flank a Bermuda longtail.
Their longtail pennants.

XIV

A barracuda
is eating a small nurse shark.
Each smiles like Buddha.

XV

What we knew as scutch
back home is "Bermuda grass."
A crutch is a crutch.

XVI

The hagfish will lunge
up an unsuspecting bum
for a plunder-plunge.

XVII

A drunken girl blabs
how *he* had put in an oar
but *she* caught a crab.

XVIII

Matted twigs and moss.
Herons turn copper-blue eggs.
Boys play pitch and toss.

XIX

Planning a furrow
right round the world, the cahow
stirs in its burrow.

XX

Tied to the drift rails
and flogged with a bull's pizzle,
a sailor still wails.

XXI

Each must make its mark.
Under my nail is a skelf
of palmetto bark.

XXII

A slap on the ass
from Hurricane Fabian
as he made a pass.

XXIII

Seigneur Cymbal slums
with a piano trio.
Park that chewing gum.

XXIV

O sole mio.
My unsalvageable sun.
O sole mio.

XXV

The cutting-room floor
is covered with bladder wrack.
The sea wind's film score.

XXVI

A horse drank the dregs
of the barrel of black rum
and found its sea legs.

XXVII

Jellyfish. Port bow.
Charms against drowning. Shipwreck.
Cauls, or "sillyhows."

XXVIII

The flash. The fizzle.
Nothing dampens a damp squib
like a rum swizzle.

XXIX

Wasp nest on the shelf?
Or a papier-mâché
maquette of itself?

XXX

The Arabian
constantly raising the bar.
Its penis-paean.

XXXI

The eel's stocking's run.
And her topmost shirt button?
Also come undone.

XXXII

Wessex saddlebacks.
The unrestricted palette
of white upon black.

XXXIII

Come come, Tom. Come come.
You know the rod spurns its root
as a rule of thumb.

XXXIV

Deck chairs on the deck.
The by-a-length teenagers
are now neck and neck.

XXXV

Hayseed hair. Sweat bib.
The otherworldly mower
rests on his scythe nib.

XXXVI

A red snail's sashay
across a desk. Sealing wax.
George III's cachet.

XXXVII

You're still Registrar
of the Admiralty docks.
Some ha'p'orth of tar.

XXXVIII

The sea's a glutton.
Just look how it's swallowed whole
that leg-o'-mutton.

XXXIX

Even the gray sole
has a migratory eye.
Even the gray sole.

XL

Bullet or ballot?
The Admiralty Court mace
is still a mallet.

XLI

Still the raw recruits.
Portuguese men-o'-war test
their new parachutes.

XLII

The sun, I'll wager,
still leaving under a cloud.
Old whiskey gauger.

XLIII

The puff-cheeked rower
rotates his oar's water globe.
Puff-cheeked *glassblower*.

XLIV

The worm that attacks
my large intestine has cut
me a little slack.

XLV

A calabash knocks
on another calabash.
This place really rocks.

XLVI

The skink, by the by,
will give you its bright blue tail.
It promised the sky.

XLVII

Through your carapace,
reports of irregularities
reaching you apace.

XLVIII

Once a lichened breast
turning from lake to lilac
was the litmus test.

XLIX

I've tested the crowd
with my elbow. Body heat.
All you've disavowed.

L

Ever technophobes,
those fireflies down and dirty
in the disco strobe.

LI

The sput-sputter-sput
where the idling fish torcher
lights on halibut.

LII

Brash, though. Brash, brash, brash.
The tree frog that weighs no more
than your cigar ash.

LIII

That thumb on the scale
of the knight's marble breastplate?
An "extinct" land snail.

LIV

We may overstate
the resemblance between us
and the clearnose skate.

LV

What disparity?
The one that beggars belief.
That disparity.

LVI

Bindweed, or smilax.
The bundle of elm branches
vindicates the ax.

LVII

They've filled their offbeat
barometers with shark oil.
Watched for the shark fleet.

LVIII

Twenty or thirty
squid have given up their ink
for this one *Certes*.

LIX

Another scorcher.
The porcelain's ohs-and-ahs
from water torture.

LX

When Malachi wore
the collar of gold. Church Bay.
A glint of foreshore.

LXI

Or the igneous
that's steeped in ignominy.
(See Vesuvius.)

LXII

Or the hidden reef
on which all authors founder.
Your agent's a thief.

LXIII

Plum-blossom blanches
at the thought of hard-gotten
plum avalanches.

LXIV

Not until the Moyle
gives back should we pay our "debt"
to our native soil.

LXV

Note how the shrimp sink
keeps the greater flamingo
in the very pink.

LXVI

Nostalgie de la
boue la boue la boue la boue:
an all-Ireland fleadh.

LXVII

Here the tree frogs play
your Melodies on fiddle,
flute-douce, flagcolet.

LXVIII

Those whin-whin-whinnies
deep in the Debtors' Prison?
Six thousand guineas.

LXIX

The sun's not risen.
Convolvulus firing squads
priming their frizzens.

LXX

One more propounder
of bottom-up management,
the rainbow flounder.

LXXI

The eel's forgotten
why around his finger's wound
a thread of cotton.

LXXII

"You mean flageo*let*.
You don't mean a kidney bean.
You mean flageo*let*."

LXXIII

Candied, by jingo,
the root of the sea holly.
Candied eryngo.

LXXIV

Orange overshoes
make the puffin less nimble
on dry land, it's true.

LXXV

Skirts round their middles,
the girls have a right confab
while taking widdles.

LXXVI

The glides and glissades
of Sir Mortimer Blenny.
That total slime-wad.

LXXVII

Guess what Easter meant
to horse-mad May and Myrtle.
A three-day event.

LXXVIII

Old burial ground.
That otherworldly scythe swish
still the only sound.

LXXIX

The dance floor's nankeen.
Still the out-at-heel drum kit
standing for the Queen.

LXXX

A predawn volley
of shots, bottoms up, chin-chin,
from the drinks trolley.

LXXXI

The seamstress thimble
seems to have taken a shine
to Seigneur Cymbal.

LXXXII

Dawn. The horseshoe crabs
have again ridden roughshod
over the blood labs.

LXXXIII

They've no antennae.
But their copper corpuscles
are two a penny.

LXXXIV

Each zebra mussel
sending the same cablegram:
HUSTLE STOP HUSTLE

LXXXV

Half-haul. Half-hurtle.
Another night on the tiles
for the sea turtle.

LXXXVI

In the petri dish
of itself the oyster, shucks,
seems quite standoffish.

LXXXVII

The butterfly sits,
another toffee-nosed toff,
on a pile of shit.

LXXXVIII

Pulsars, Tom. Spin-spin.
Even the moon's novelty
has worn a bit thin.

LXXXIX

The glass of red wine
with which I saw eye to eye
until half past nine.

XC

Completely at odds.
We're now completely at odds.
Completely at odds.

RIDDLE

My first may be found, if found it ever is, quite firmly embedded in grime
but not in rime,
despite the fact that I'm
cold as well as dirty, what with being stowed away almost all the time.

My second sounds doubly in roar
and singly in oar.
When the buccaneers put ashore
and set fire to our little craft, my spirit would sink, then soar

when I thought of my third, found in the ideal
but not in the raw deal
I got from them. Just because I've a heart of steel
doesn't mean I don't *feel*.

My fourth is in Drake
but not in rake.
They'd rake the coals they'd make me walk. My last request was for a
        steak
followed by something like a piece of cake.

My fifth is in drum
but not in rum.
The drunken buccaneers offered me a lump of dough if I'd keep mum.
A lump in my throat. My lump sum.

My sixth is in leaves
but not in eaves.
I overheard them laughing about "honour among thieves"
when they left me stranded here with the dry heaves.

My last heaves to, as it were, twice in event
but once only in vent.
I'm still wearing that old stovepipe hat. I've made scarcely a dent
in that lump of dough I was given, or lent,

by the buccaneers from whom I still take my cue.
A barb of smoke from the barbecue
brings a blush to the cheek of the cockatoo
who'll wait as long for a word from me as I'll wait for a word from you.

TURKEY BUZZARDS

They've been so long above it all,
        those two petals
so steeped in style they seem to stall
        in the kettle

simmering over the town dump
        or, better still,
the neon-flashed, X-rated rump
        of fresh roadkill

courtesy of the interstate
        that Eisenhower
would overtake in the home straight
        by one horsepower,

the kettle where it all boils down
        to the thick scent
of death, a scent of such renown
        it's given vent

to the idea buzzards can spot
        a deer carcass
a mile away, smelling the rot
        as, once, Marcus

Aurelius wrinkled his nose
        at a gas leak
from the Great Sewer that ran through Rome
        to the Tiber

then went searching out, through the gloam,
        one subscriber

to the other view that the rose,
      full-blown, antique,

its no-frills ruff, the six-foot shrug
      of its swing-wings,
the theologian's and the thug's
      twin triumphings

in a buzzard's shaved head and snood,
      buzz-buzz-buzzy,
its logic in all likelihood
      somewhat fuzzy,

would ever come into focus,
      it ever deign
to dispense its hocus-pocus
      in that same vein

as runs along an inner thigh
      to where, too right,
the buzzard vouchsafes not to shy
      away from shite,

its mission not to give a miss
      to a bête noire,
all roly-poly, full of piss
      and vinegar,

trying rather to get to grips
      with the grommet
of the gut, setting its tinsnips
      to that grommet

in the spray-painted hind's hindgut
and making a
sweeping, too right, a sweeping cut
that's so blasé

it's hard to imagine, dear Sis,
why others shrink
from this sight of a soul in bliss,
so in the pink

from another month in the red
of the shambles,
like a rose in over its head
among brambles,

unflappable in its belief
it's Ararat
on which the Ark would come to grief,
abjuring that

Marcus Aurelius humbug
about what springs
from earth succumbing to the tug
at its heartstrings,

reported to live past fifty,
as you yet may,
dear Sis, perhaps growing your hair
in requital,

though briefly, of whatever tears
at your vitals,

learning, perhaps, from the nifty,
      nay *thrifty*, way

these buzzards are given to stoop
      and take their ease
by letting their time-chastened poop
      fall to their knees

till they're almost as bright with lime
      as their night roost,
their poop containing an enzyme
      that's known to boost

their immune systems, should they prong
      themselves on small
bones in a cerebral cortex,
      at no small cost

to their well-being, sinking fast
      in a deer crypt,
buzzards getting the hang at last
      of being stripped

of their command of the vortex
      while having lost
their common touch, they've been so long
      above it all.

STARLINGS, BROAD STREET, TRENTON, 2003

Indiscernible, for the most part, the welts and weals
on their two-a-penny skins,
weals got by tinkering with tin-
foil from condoms or chewing gum, welts as slow to heal

as spot-welds on steel
in a chop shop where, by dint of the din,
their calls will be no clearer than their colors till they spin
(or are spun) around to reveal

this other sphere in which their hubbub's the hubbub
of all-night revelers at reveille,
girls with shoes in hand, boys giving their all

to the sidewalk outside a club,
their gloom a gloom so distinctly shot through with glee
they might be dancing still under a disco ball.

THE COYOTE

Veering down the track like a girl veering down a cobbled street
in the meatpacking district,
high heels from the night before, black shawl of black-tipped hairs,

steering clear of that fluorescent ring
spray-painted on an even stretch of blacktop
like a ring in which we might once have played keepsies,

veering down the track without the slightest acknowledgement from
    Angus,
the dog lying in a heap on our porch
like a heap of clothes lying beside a bed,

Angus who had himself been found wandering by the highway
somewhere on the far side of Lake Champlain,
slubber-furred, slammerkin, backbone showing through,

and, though we didn't know it when we brought him home,
blind in one eye, the right one,
the one between him and the coyote,

the cloudy, flaw-fleckered marble of that eye
now turning on you and me,
taking in the spray-painted ring where you and I knuckle down.

NOW PITCHING HIMSELF LIKE A FORLORN HOPE

Now pitching himself like a forlorn hope
in a pitched battle, Angus howls and howls
from his heavy-duty berserker cowl,
his hound voice not quite managing to cope

with his not quite having managed to brace
himself against this latest call to arms
(as it happens, the Griggstown fire alarm),
till he does some manner of about-face

quite in step with his old messmate, Soren,
who forward lives, yes, forward lives his life
but only backward hears the police siren

articulate the exit-ramp jackknife
of a tractor-trailer, a trailer rife
with ricin or mustard gas or sarin.

PERDU

The orchard walls are high and hard to climb
and I've stood sentinel here for a long time.

A long time since I dropped down on this side
with the bow and arrows Quintus had wind-dried.

Wind-dried yew is proof against warp and mold
but not the mindfulness of a five-year-old.

My five-year-old had eyed me through and through:
"Tell the buriers to bury me with you."

With me he'd learn the ways of the yew stave
a Salish man might bring with him to the grave.

The grave already held two powder kegs
and I came to as they were breaking my legs.

They were breaking my legs so I would fit
when I came to and called for an end to it.

An end to the ration of bread and beer
and the rationale for having dropped me here.

They dropped me here still bloody from the "scratch"
I might have got from a shadowy Sasquatch.

A shadowy Sasquatch from Klamath Falls
who might be set on scaling the orchard walls.

The orchard walls are high and hard to climb
and I've stood sentinel here for a long time.

THE LANDING

A full moon. A squid hauling itself through knee-deep shallows.
Its shadow-skite along the seabed
easily mistaken, wee one, for the unabashedness
of an amphibious vehicle
armed with a .50 caliber Browning machine gun,
the tank exonerating itself from the carrier
easily mistaken for a truck
off-loading blankets and medicine,
the truck so easily mistaken for the divan
on which we've made another hand-over-fist
attempt to cover our asses
and leave some wiggle room.
A full moon, wee one. The squid flutters some kind of belly-hatch.
It shines a beam on the seabed to cancel its own shadow.

THE MOUNTAIN IS HOLDING OUT

The mountain is holding out
for news from the sea
of the raid on the redoubt.
The plain won't level with me

for news from the sea
is harder and harder to find.
The plain won't level with me
now it's nonaligned

and harder and harder to find.
The forest won't fill me in
now it, too, is nonaligned
and its patience wearing thin.

The forest won't fill me in
or the lake confess
to its patience wearing thin.
I'd no more try to guess

why the lake might confess
to a regard for its own sheen,
no more try to guess
why the river won't come clean

on its regard for its own sheen
than why you and I've faced off across a ditch.
For the river not coming clean
is only one of the issues on which

you and I've faced off across a ditch
and the raid on the redoubt
only one of the issues on which
the mountain is holding out.

MEDLEY FOR MORIN KHUR

I

The sound box is made of a horse's head.
The resonator is horse skin.
The strings and bow are of horsehair.

II

The morin khur is the thoroughbred
of Mongolian violins.
Its call is the call of the stallion to the mare.

III

A call which may no more be gainsaid
than that of jinn to jinn
through jasmine-weighted air.

IV

A call that may no more be gainsaid
than that of blood kin to kin
through a body-strewn central square.

V

A square in which they'll heap the horses' heads
by the heaps of horse skin
and the heaps of horsehair.

GLAUCUS

It went without saying that a king of Corinth
should keep his prize fillies out of the fray
and, rather than have them enmesh
themselves in horse toils, horse tattle,

set them up, each on a plinth,
and fillet their manes with knots and nosegays
and feed them the choicest human flesh
to give them a taste for battle.

It went without saying that after he lost control
of his chariot team at Pelias, and made a hames
of setting them all square,

Glaucus was still on such a roll
it was lost on him that the high point of the games
was his being eaten now by his own mares.

THE LAST TIME I SAW CHRIS

In Amagansett, for crying out loud, setting the arm of his French
     helpmeet
toward a funky-as-it-gets exhibit in the Crazy Monkey,
a crosscut saw
in the window not quite making up for this not quite being Long Island
     Sound,
the gobs of tar
on his and his buddy's pants

suggesting they might have been willing participants
in some recent keelhauling. Blown, too, the opportunity to meet
and greet an incipient Jack Tar
or wannabe grease monkey
in an outhouse wired, for the love of Mike, for sound.
When he turned away from me I could have sworn I saw

a woman on a seesaw
from the seventies, still flying a flag for the seventies. That's what was
     with the hot pants.
The politest way of putting it would be to say she and I'd been trying to
     sound
each other out, though it seemed unlikely ever the twain would meet.
She was just back from Benin. No monkey
business without an overcoat, for crying out loud. No losing the ship for a
     ha'p'orth of tar.

Not ship, I was treading water. *Sheep.* A sheep being the avatar
of no god we know of, always the best kind. For she was musing on an
     ancient saw
having to do with a monkey
and paying p(e)an(u)ts

to the guide, for the love of Mike, who'd led her hunting trip. A
    hartebeest meet
summoned by a hartebeest bugle, a sound

that had barely the strength to resound
through the bush. Boots and saddles. The clench of Wright's coal tar
as she suddenly deemed it meet
to turn the other cheek, for crying out loud, looking back at me as if she
    saw that I foresaw
the needle tracks just above the line of her pants
when her arms would set from years of firing up, as if I foresaw the
    monkey

on her back (*"les ans, mon ange, les ans manqués"*),
as if I might look forward from an era in which we were all still relatively
    sound
in wind and limb to an era of night sweats, gasps, and pants,
for the love of Mike, now threatening to tar
all of us, straight or gay, with the same brush, the god who oversaw
our not knowing of him yearning now to mete

out retribution as the hartebeest pants for cooling streams, *taratantara,*
    taratantara,
our breathing indistinguishable now from the sound of a saw
through the breast of a monkey, for crying out loud, through monkey- or
    other bush-meat.

HEDGE SCHOOL

Not only those rainy mornings our great-great-grandmother was posted at
    a gate
with a rush mat
over her shoulders, a mat that flashed
Papish like a heliograph, but those rainy mornings when my daughter and
    the rest

of her all-American Latin class may yet be forced to conjugate
Guantánamo, amas, amat
and learn with Luciana how "headstrong liberty is lash'd
with woe"—all past and future mornings were impressed

on me just now, dear Sis,
as I sheltered in a doorway on Church Street in St. Andrews
(where, in 673, another Maelduin was bishop),

and tried to come up with a ruse
for unsealing the *New Shorter Oxford English Dictionary* back in that corner
    shop
and tracing the root of *metastasis.*

SILLYHOW STRIDE

In memory of Warren Zevon

I

I want you to tell me if, on Grammy night, you didn't get one hell of a
    kick
out of all those bling-it-ons in their bulletproof broughams,
all those line managers who couldn't manage a line of coke,

all those Barmecides offering beakers of barm—
if you didn't get a kick out of being as incongruous
there as John Donne at a junior prom.

Two graves must hide, Warren, thine and mine corse
who, on the day we met, happened
also to meet an individual dragging a full-length cross

along 42nd Street and kept mum, each earning extra Brownie points
for letting that cup pass. The alcoholic
knows that to enter in these bonds

is to be free, yeah right. The young John Donne who sets a Glock
on his dish in the cafeteria
knows that, even as he plots to clean some A & R man's clock,

his muse on dromedary
trots to the Indias of spice and mine
and the Parsi Towers of Silence, even as he buses his tray

with its half-eaten dish of beef chow mein
to the bus station, he's already gone halfway to meet the Space Lab.
The *Space* Lab (italics mine),

where you worked on how many mint juleps
it takes to make a hangover
while playing piano for all those schlubs you could eclipse

and cloud with a wink. I long to talk to some old lover's
ghost about the night after night you tipped the scales
for the Everly Brothers,

Frank and Jesse, while learning to inhale
through a French inhaler like a child soldier from the Ivory Coast
learning to parch a locust on a machete, a child soldier who would e-mail

you, at your request,
a copy of "Death Be Not Proud," a child soldier who would Hi-Lite
a locust with a flame. If your grave be broke up again some second guest

to entertain, let it serve as hallowed
ground where those young shavers
from the Ivory Coast may find their careers, as you found yours, on hold,

where Tim McGraw and OutKast, not to speak of those underachievers
who don a black hat or a goatee
as a computer screen dons a screen saver

or the Princeton sky its seventeen-year cicadas,
will find themselves on hold. You who went searching for a true, plain
    heart
as an unreconstructed renegade

must have come to believe, with Frank and Jesse, no hate could hurt
our bodies like our love. Another low-down
dirty shame . . . To wicked spirits horrid

shapes assigned . . . Every nickel nudging the nickelodeon.
O wrangling schools . . . O wrangling schools that search what fire
shall burn this world, had none the wit to smell Izaak Walton

pressing down on Donne's funeral pyre,
yeah right, to smell the locust parched by that Ivory Coast subaltern,
had none the wit unto this knowledge to aspire,

that this *your* fever, the fever that still turns
the turntable, might be it? For every turn, like every tuning, is open,
every thorn a durian,

every *bin* a *ben*
on the outskirts of Jerusalem. Such a pilgrimage were sweet,
Warren, barreling down the autobahn

through West Hollywood
in your little black Corvette (part barge,
part-hermaphrodite brig), our eyes set not on the noted weed

but the noted *seaweed* of Nobu Matsuhisa. Those child soldiers who parch
a locust on a machete while tending a .50 caliber
Browning with a dodgy breech

will know how the blood labors
to beget Matsuhisa-san's seared *toro*. At the winter solstice, as I filed
past a band of ticket scalpers

who would my ruined fortune flout
at Madison Square Garden, I glimpsed a man in a Tibetan
cap, nay-saying a flute,

whom I took at first to be an older Brian Jones, what with his flipping a butane
lighter in my face and saying, "I shall be made thy music . . ."
At that very moment, quite unbidden,

the ghost of Minoru Yamasaki
(who had trailed me from the bar at Nobu), exhorted me to "Turn them speakers
up full blast now *Lucies*, who scarce seven hours herself unmasks,

is sunk so low as my Twin Towers . . ." Brian Jones's patent winkle-pickers
reflected a patent sky. "All strange wonders that befell
me while the rest of them recorded *Beggars*

Banquet and I was sunk so low in Twickenham, lovers coming with crystal vials
to take my tears . . ." "I'll do my crying in the rain
with Don and Phil,"

said Yamasaki-san, "I'll do my crying with Frank and Jesse waiting for a train . . .
Those lines you wrote about the bloodbath
at my Twin Towers, about the sky being full of carrion,

those were *my* Twin Towers, right?" Brian, meanwhile, continued to puff
on the flute as if he were indeed corporeal,
as if he were no less substantial than the elder-pith

nay on which he played a hurry home early
version of "Walk Right Back," the "Walk Right Back"
you yourself had played night after night with Frank and Jesse Everly.

II

I knelt beside my sister's bed, Warren, the valleys and the peaks
of the EKGs, the crepusculine X-rays,
the out-of-date blister packs

discarded by those child soldiers from the Ivory Coast or Zaire,
and couldn't think that she had sunk so low
she might not make the anniversary

of our mother's death from this same cancer, this same quick, quick, slow
conversion of manna to gall
from which she died thirty years ago. I knelt and adjusted the sillyhow

of her oxygen mask, its vinyl caul
unlikely now to save Maureen from drowning in her own spit.
I thought of how the wrangling schools

need look no further than her bed
to find what fire shall burn this world—or that heaven
which "is one with" this world—to find how gold to airy thinness beat

may crinkle like cellophane
in a flame, like cellophane or the flimmerings of gauze
by which a needle is held fast in a vein.

So break off, Warren, break off this last lamenting kiss
as Christ broke with Iscariot
and gave himself to those loosey-goosey

Whisky A Go Going mint julep– and margarita-
and gimlet-grinders, those gin fizz-
iognomists. My first guitar, a Cort, and my first amp, a Crate,

I myself had tried to push through a Fuzz Face
or some shit-kicking stomp box
till I blew every fuse

in Central New Jersey. At the autumnal equinox
as on St. Lucies when sunbeams in the east are spread
I'd pretend the Crate was a Vox

AC-50 Super Twin. I was playing support
for some star in the unchangeable firmament
in which the flesh, Warren, is merely a bruise on the spirit,

a warm-up for the main event
as the hymnal ushers in the honky-tonk
or the oxygen tent

raises the curtain on the oxygen mask. How well you knew that dank
spot on the outskirts
of Jerusalem where the kids still squeeze between the tanks

to suck the life out of a cigarette,
the maple bud in spring like something coming to a head,
some pill that can't be sugared,

another hit
of hooch or horse that double-ties the subtile knot
to which we've paid so little heed

all those years of running amuck in Kent.
Go tell court huntsmen that the oxygen-masked King will ride
ten thousand days and nights

on a stride piano, yeah right,
through the hell in which Ignatius of "Ignatius His Conclave"
was strung out on Mandrax and mandrake root,

ten thousand nights of the "chemical life"
(as Auden styled it, turning the speakers up full blast),
the "chemical life" that gives way to ten thousand days of rehab and golf

in the afternoon, televangelists,
push up and bench press with Buddhist and Parsi,
ten thousand days after which you realized

the flesh is indeed no more than a bruise
on the spirit. The werewolf with the Japanese menu in his hand,
keen as he was to show his prowess

with the chopsticks, realized it ain't
that pretty, ain't that pretty at all
to be completely wasted when you're testing your chops, hint hint,

on a Gibson Les Paul
overdriven through a Fender Vibratone,
ain't that pretty to crawl

to Ensenada for methadone.
Were we not weaned till then from Mandrax and mandrake
or snorted we in the seven sleepers' den

a line of coke, or wore long sleeves to cover the wreak
of injecting diacetylmorphine?
I was playing a Fender through a Marshall rig

that was so massively overdriven
I couldn't hear the phone ring, didn't hear that excitable boy
extol the virtues of Peruvian

over Bolivian marching powder, that excitable *hula-hula* boy,
the Jackson Browne sound-alike,
who waited on us in Nobu (Nobu or Koi?)

where the fishionistas [*sic*] walked the catwalk
for as long as they could manage a line
of coke with their sushi deluxe,

for as long as they were able for the baby abalone
with garlic sauce. We watched those two Parascenders parascend
off Malibu like two true, plain

hearts who struggle to fend
off the great crash—two true, plain hearts like yourself and Maureen
who struggled to fend off the great crash that has us end

where we began, all strung out on heroin
on the outskirts of La Caldera,
our last few grains of heroin ash stashed in a well-wrought urn.

III

I want you to tell me, Warren, if you didn't watch those two hang gliders
and think of the individual we saw drag
his full-length cross through the under-the-counter culture

of 42nd Street? 42nd or Canal? A certain individual, whatreck,
who might easily have taken in a 4 a.m. show at the Clark and got to
    grips
with the usherette's leg in the dark,

who might have recognized the usherette for a certain demirep
who'd registered her domain
in the Adelphi, having already learned the ropes

from the old bluesmen
who played in the Blue Note. That must have been your first brush
with greatness, in Chicago, before the mean

streets of L.A. where your Moses met the bulrush
of Stravinsky and every chord became a cordon sanitaire
against the bum's rush

your Russian Jewish father had given you in Culver and Century
Cities, your G major seeing his G major
in gloves-off gambling, and though music did in the center

sit right through that *Wanderjahre*
with Stravinsky, I'm certain it would also lean and hearken
after the jubilation and the jeers

of the boxing ring in which your father took on some cocksure Puerto
    Rican,
in which every Baby Grand cried out for a Crybaby
and the Everlasting Life we bargain

for was invented by some record company pooh-bah
who has forgotten, in the midst of things,
that every operation's mom-and-pop,

your Scottish Mormon mother teaching you the right swing
against your father's left, your common
G on the Chickering

sounding against the G-men
who plagued him about that pyramid scheme he set up in the Faeroes
with Mr. Cambio and Mr. Gombeen.

I want you to tell me if grief, brought to numbers, cannot be so fierce,
pace Donne's sales pitch,
for he tames, that fetters it in verse,

throwing up a last ditch
against the mounted sorrows, for I have more, Warren, I have more,
more as an even flame two hearts did touch

and left us mere
philosophers whose blood still labors to beget
child-soldiers toasting locust s'mores,

the A & R men lining their pockets
while Roland battled the Bantu to their knees,
the Bantu who boogie-woogied

with Saint Ignatius
through their post-traumatic stress disorder,
the Les Paul pushed through a Pignose

like a, yeah right, RotoRooter
through a sewage line, the A & R men taking the mazuma
and crossing the border

to load up on sashimi
with Yamasaki-san, a headless Childe Roland
coming to his dark twin Towers of Silence, zoom zoom,

those Towers the Parsis still delineate
as scaffolds for sky burial, a quorum
of vultures letting their time-chastened lant

fall to their knees as they hold on like grim
death to the bellied-up Brian Jones, their office indulgently to fit
actives to passives in the doldrums

of the swimming pool, the fishionistas (*q.v.*) with their food fads
having nothing on these rare
birds that divide

the spoils, Warren, these rare
birds that divide the spoils
with the gasbag, gobshite, gumptionless A & R

men who couldn't tell a hollow-body Les Paul with double-coil
pickups pushed through a Princeton Reverb
from a slab of London broil

an excitable boy might rub
all over his chest, the vultures working piecemeal
at his chest like the chest on which a Russian Jewish cardsharp

and a Scottish Mormon broke the seal
as surely as one V.I.P. opening her bosom made one Viper Room
an everywhere, every Glock sighing for a glockenspiel,

every frame a freeze-frame
of two alcoholics barreling down to Ensenada
in a little black Corvette, vroom vroom,

for Diet, yeah right, *Diet* Mountain Dew,
that individual carrying his cross knowing the flesh is a callus
on the spirit as surely as you knew the mesotheliomata

on both lungs meant the situation was lose-lose,
every full-length cross carrier almost certainly up to some sort of high
    jinks
else a great Prince in prison lies,

lies belly-up on a Space Lab scaffold where the turkey buzzards pink
Matsuhisa-san's seared *toro*,
turkey buzzards waiting for you to eclipse and cloud them with a wink

as they hold out their wings and of the sun his working vigor borrow
before they parascend through the Viper Room or the Whisky A Go Go,
each within its own "cleansing breeze," its own *Cathartes aura.*

ACKNOWLEDGMENTS

Acknowledgments are due to the editors of *Agenda, Aquarius, The Best American Poetry 2004, The Best American Poetry 2006, Boston College Magazine, Botteghe Oscure, Cimarron Review, Columbia Magazine, Cork Literary Review, Crowd, Five Points, Fulcrum, Gulf Coast, Irish Pages, Journal of Irish Studies, Lily, Limestone, Metre, Modern Haiku, The New York Times, Octopus, Painted Bride Quarterly, Parapet, PEN America, PN Review, Poetry Daily, Poetry Ireland Review, Poetry London, The Recorder, River City, Smartish Pace, Tatler, The Threepenny Review, TLS, turnrow,* and *Verse.*

"Tithonus," "Soccer Moms," "At Least They Weren't Speaking French," "Turkey Buzzards," "The Landing," and "The Last Time I Saw Chris" appeared in *The New Yorker.*

"Bob Dylan at Princeton, November 2000" was included in *"Do You, Mr. Jones?" Bob Dylan with the Poets and Professors* (Chatto and Windus), "Soccer Moms" in *180 More: Extraordinary Poems for Every Day* (Random House), "The Treaty" in *Out of Fashion: An Anthology of Poems* (Faber and Faber), "Eggs" in *New Writing 14* (Granta), "Medley for Morin Khur" in *Something Beginning with P: New Poems from Irish Poets* (O'Brien Press), "Glaucus" in *Wild Reckoning: An Anthology Provoked by Rachel Carson's Silent Spring* (Calouste Gulbenkian Foundation), and "Hedge School" in *The Book of St Andrews: An Anthology* (Polygon). An earlier version of "Horse Latitudes," along with "Medley for Morin Khur," was published in a limited edition by Enitharmon Press under the title *Medley for Morin Khur,* while a version of "90 Instant Messages to Tom Moore" was published by Modern Haiku Press as *Sixty Instant Messages to Tom Moore.* Section I of "The Old Country" was published as an Oxford Poetry Broadside, "The Coyote" by Sutton Hoo Press, "Now Pitching Himself Like a Forlorn Hope" by Baylor University Press, and "The Mountain Is Holding Out" by the Yeats Society Sligo. "It Is What It Is" was published in a limited edition by Peter Fallon/Gallery Press in December 2005.